"In this devotional book, Hilarie has captured some of the most important topics that single mothers deal with. Single mothers struggle with finding Scriptures that fit their daily situations. There are times when they feel the Bible is not structured for single mothers. Hilarie was able to find the right Scriptures and words to connect with me. The words gave me hope that (1) I was not the only one feeling this way and (2) God sees me and has a plan for any issue that I am dealing with. The devotionals are short and to the point. I recommend this devotional book not just to single mothers but to all mothers. I can't wait till this book is released."

—**Trasa Richmond,**
Veteran, mother of three

"I was blessed with Hilarie's friendship during a difficult and challenging time in my life. Her friendship, wisdom, and unfailing love for God provided me with the guidance I needed to cope with a life-changing transition. She continues to feed my soul with Scriptures that resonate during times when I lack hope. Hilarie has faced challenges beyond my personal threshold of resilience, but her love for God remained strong, and she was determined to persevere regardless of her circumstances. She is a fierce and compassionate woman with a heart that overflows with love for others. This love is captured in her devotional and presented to you as encouragement to find peace, strength, and love in our heavenly Father."

—**Angie B.-E.,**
Mother, student, and daughter of the King

"The Scripture is spot on, and Hilarie's comments are sincere and relatable even for someone who is not a single mom. This devotional also brings such an awareness of how much all mothers shoulder on a daily basis. Hilarie's strength is inspiring and encouraging to say the least. As she writes about how much mothers are required to pour out for others every day, I love the analogy that this book is a respite for single moms to fill their cups back up so they can pour out again tomorrow. I love how Hilarie leaves space for thanksgiving and gratitude as it is imperative that we acknowledge even the smallest of blessings. Thanksgiving can completely change my mindset for that day, week, and month. Hilarie, I am so proud of your efforts!"

—**Lauren H.,**
Married, mother of three

"In her writing, you can feel that Hilarie is a child of God. Her devotion is evident every day in her words and actions. And we are all so fortunate that she has chosen to share pieces of herself and her journey with us. Even if you're not a single mother, you can find wisdom, comfort, and inspiration in this devotional, and for that, Hilarie, I thank you."

—**Kristel Brown,**
Friend

Girl, *He's Got You*

A Single Mother's Devotional

Hilarie Rock

LUCIDBOOKS

Girl, He's Got You
A Single Mother's Devotional

Copyright © 2021 by Hilarie Rock

Published by Lucid Books in Houston, TX
www.lucidbookspublishing.com

All rights reserved. No part of this publication may be reproduced, stored in a retrieval system, or transmitted in any form by any means, electronic, mechanical, photocopy, recording, or otherwise, without the prior permission of the publisher, except as provided for by USA copyright law.

Unless otherwise indicated, all Scripture quotations are taken from the Holy Bible, New International Version®, NIV®. Copyright © 1973, 1978, 1984, 2011 by Biblica, Inc.™ Used by permission of Zondervan. All rights reserved worldwide. www.zondervan.com The "NIV" and "New International Version" are trademarks registered in the United States Patent and Trademark Office by Biblica, Inc.™

Scripture quotations marked (ESV) are taken from the ESV® Bible (The Holy Bible, English Standard Version®), copyright © 2001 by Crossway, a publishing ministry of Good News Publishers. Used by permission. All rights reserved.

eISBN: 978-1-63296-437-3
ISBN: 978-1-63296-436-6

Special Sales: Most Lucid Books titles are available in special quantity discounts. Custom imprinting or excerpting can also be done to fit special needs. For standard bulk orders, go to www.lucidbooksbulk.com. For specialty press or large orders, contact Lucid Books at books@lucidbookspublishing.com.

This book is dedicated to Larry Gene George—the man I prayed for, the man God sent to encourage and love me, the faithful servant He called home before any of us were ready.

Table of Contents

Foreword	ix
Preface	xi
Introduction	1

Emotional Matters	**3**
Loneliness	5
Fear	9
Anger	14
Feeling Like a Failure	18
Hate	22
Being Frustrated	26
Heartache	30
Forgiveness	34
Pride	38
Letting Love In	42
The Other Parent	46
Feeling Safe	50
Fear of Dying	54

Personal Matters	**59**
Judgment from Society	61
Friendships	65
Taking Care of Yourself	69
Realizing What Is Important	73
Death and Dying	77
Dating	82
Blame Game	86
Ashamed of Our Failures	90
Guilt and Shame	94

Self-Worth	98
Difficult Family	102
Not Having Enough	106
Legal Battles	110

Practical Matters — **115**

Making Ends Meet	117
Balancing It All	121
Discipline	125
Sex	129
Mentors for Your Children	133
Our Mentors	137
Being Deceived	142
Making Hard Decisions	146
Time Management	151
Exercise	156

Matters of Faith — **161**

Lies of the Enemy	163
Unanswered Prayers	167
How to Begin/Revive a Prayer Life	171
Idols	175
God's Gifts	179
Integrity	185
Surrender to the Lord	189
Serving	195
God First	199

Acknowledgments	205
Notes	207

Foreword

According to one paraphrase of Luke 12:49, Jesus tells his followers that *great gifts mean great responsibilities.*

This uplifting, six-week devotional demonstrates the power of Jesus's words. Hilarie Rock has been deeply loved through her challenging journey as a single mom. We have seen and recognized God's goodness to her all along the way, and she is eager to share with others what He has given her.

We are grateful she has determined to focus on those in her same place in life—single motherhood. Through her challenges as a single mom, she has experienced firsthand what we all should know and embrace: that daily spiritual sustenance from His written word is essential. Hilarie especially knows and communicates that the grounding of all wisdom is in the gracious gospel of Jesus—the forgiveness we find in His life, death, and resurrection.

It has been a blessing to watch Hilarie grow and mature in her desire to bring God glory in whatever she does (1 Corinthians 10:31). It is our prayer that this devotional—written from her heart—will indeed bring Him great glory.

Michael and Christy Boys

Dr. Michael Boys is the former lead teaching pastor at Christ Community Church (C3) in Houston, Texas. He is currently lead teaching pastor at Calvary Baptist Church in Santa Barbara, California.

Preface

I have been a single mother since my son, Mitchell, was born. I knew from day one that I would be the decision maker and breadwinner for the long haul. But somewhere in the recesses of my mind, I just knew that Prince Charming would come along and save me. I got close to getting that happily-ever-after some of us seek, but God called him home before we were officially engaged. Fourteen years later, I am still a single parent. But I am not bitter, depressed, or alone. I may not be married, but I have someone bigger—I have God! My walk is like many other Christians' walks. I have fallen many times, but I continue to get up and try again. I am not perfect, nor am I striving for perfection. I just want to finish well.

> *His master replied, "Well done, good and faithful servant! You have been faithful with a few things; I will put you in charge of many things. Come and share your master's happiness!"*
> —Matt. 25:21

I have been told over the years that I make the "Single Mom" thing look easy. I've been told, "You have the best kid. I bet he never gives you any trouble." Both of those statements are nice but not true. What I have is God, what I do is pray, and what I am is a daughter of the King. That statement is in no way meant to shame anyone or make you think I am perfect. My walk with the Lord started almost a decade before Mitchell was born. The woman encouraging me should have given up. She poured into me; I took and walked away. This cycle continued for many years. I grew up in the church, but I had no idea that we could *all* have a personal and rich relationship with our Lord and Savior Jesus

Christ. The same woman who encouraged me for that decade shared the following Scripture with me:

> *"For I know the plans I have for you," declares the* LORD, *"plans to prosper you and not to harm you, plans to give you a hope and a future."*
> —Jer. 29:11

I carried this verse around in my wallet or purse for years. Whenever I truly felt I needed help and prayer, I would put it in my pocket, so it would be closer to me. After about five years, I left it in a pair of jeans that went through the wash. I was devastated! In my hurt and disappointment at myself I realized that I had committed the verse to memory; the piece of paper it was written on was merely sentimental. You can hide God's Word in your heart and always have it with you.

> *I have hidden your word in my heart.*
> —Ps. 119:11

Fast-forward about 10 years, and that same friend encouraged me to attend a moms' Bible study. Mitchell was about 18 months old. I went, but I did *not* want to go. Every mom looked different from me; everyone was married, and they all seemed to have it together. Man, I could not have been more wrong! I befriended two women who helped me in my walk, one of whom is *still* encouraging me to this day.

Knowing that I was a new Christian, they encouraged and helped me in my struggle to be a good mom, friend, family member, and Christian. It took a while, but I finally began my walk with the Lord. It is never too late to start or restart. You are never too old. The Lord wants you like no other. He desires your worship and your praise.

> *I am the vine; you are the branches. Whoever abides in me and I in him, he it is that bears much fruit, for apart from me you can do nothing.*
> —John 15:5 ESV

Preface

This book was inspired by single mothers and mentors in my life who are constantly pouring into me so that I may encourage others. It is a series of encouraging Scriptures. Although single motherhood is the hardest journey I have ever taken, it is also one of the most rewarding. However, please know I struggled; I still struggle. I must constantly renew and refresh my mind with God's Word. I am human, and so are you! Give yourself some grace, for God is always showing us His incredible grace and mercy.

> *For it is by grace you have been saved, through faith—and this is not from yourselves, it is the gift of God—not by works, so that no one can boast.*
> —Eph. 2:8–9

As a single mother and the child of a single mother, I have faced all the challenges I mention in this devotional and then some. But I've learned that although we single moms are solo parents, we are *never* alone. God is always in our hearts and closer to situations than you might imagine. All things are done for His glory.

> *The Lord is close to the brokenhearted and saves those who are crushed in spirit.*
> —Ps. 34:18

The Scripture I'd carried in my purse for years was one way I practiced leaning on God. That verse encouraged me when I was discouraged, strengthened me when I felt weak, gave me hope when I was in despair. Your way of leaning on God may look different, but my hope is to provide you with the tools needed to replace the fear, lies, doubt, or despair with truth—truth from God's Word. In this book, I have included problems and dilemmas familiar to single mothers and used Scripture to strengthen the spirit, provide hope, and encourage.

> *The Lord will guide you always; he will satisfy your needs in a sun-scorched land and will strengthen your frame. You will be like a well-watered garden, like a spring whose waters never fail.*
> —Isa. 58:11

Introduction

This devotional is for single mothers. It has 45 days of Scripture paired with the unique challenges that single mothers face, plus additional Scripture to dig deeper. After each reading, I have provided thought-provoking questions that get the shovel digging.

While the task of single parenting is daunting and many times painful and difficult, God has not left us to be a solo act. We are designed to be in constant contact with Him, asking for His help with our every need.

This devotional and subsequent questions are designed to help single mothers depend more on our Lord and Savior and less on the world we live in. It is also intended to help reset, restart, and renew our walk with Jesus. We are His adopted heirs and daughters to His kingdom. Many days, we do not feel like heirs. Many of us have never been told we are beautiful, worthy, or heirs of a heavenly kingdom, nor have we been treated as a princess. But we are. It says so in His Word.

> *Daughters of kings are among your honored women.*
> —Ps. 45:9

Once we realize who we are in Christ, we look and act differently—because we are *His*! What a wonderful treasure to pass down to our sons and daughters. To know the love of Christ and to be counted as one of His own is one of the greatest gifts you can give a child. It is never too late to renew your commitment to our precious Lord and Savior.

I am by no means a preacher or biblical scholar. I do not profess to know the Bible backward and forward. I am an average person; however, I have above average mentors and women of God who pour into me their encouragement, love, knowledge of Scripture, and teaching. They guide, support, and help me renew my faith in a way that allows me to turn around and give others what I have been given. That is the beauty of Christ. Once you get this amazing gift, you want to give it away to as many people as possible and share the good news of the gospel.

The design of the book is simple. Each topic begins with an example of what we, as single mothers, face in the world. Then there is Scripture to rely on in that situation. The third component includes godly questions to ask yourself. Answering them is where the hard work in your heart will begin to change your attitude. The internal change you experience will alter how each situation affects you and ultimately how you show the world Christ through your actions.

Emotional Matters

Life as a single mom feels as if it is one continuous emotional roller coaster. Even with a strong faith, we seem to ride the never-ending wave of emotions. We are up and down and in and out with our own feelings as well as the emotions of our children. It has never been God's desires to see us falter or fail. We are His children, and He is our loving parent. He desires only the best for us.

The following devotionals address common issues we all face. I pray you find peace in knowing you are not alone. God sees us and hears us. We are His, and He is working behind the scenes to make beauty from ashes. He's got you!

> *The righteous person may have many troubles, but the Lord delivers him from them all.*
>
> —Ps. 34:19

Loneliness

Single motherhood comes with bouts of incredible loneliness. I am not speaking of feeling alone, although we feel that too. I am speaking of physical loneliness. These feelings do not discriminate. They pop up when we least expect them—in a crowd, at work, in church, or by ourselves. We usually experience this intense loneliness during storms in life. However, we are never truly alone, not if we let the Lord in. There is not a husband sitting beside us in church or at the dinner table but consider who *is* there. This is a great teaching moment for our children. Let them know that our heavenly Father is always with us.

> *Yet I am always with you: you hold me by my right hand.*
> —Ps. 73:23

Please be encouraged when I say that you are *never* alone. Yes, you will cry and feel sad, but guess what? So does every other human on the planet. Our Lord and Savior is always with you. Just call His name. Know His Word is true. His promises are for you. Your salvation is why Jesus paid the ultimate price. Let Him fill in the lonely moments. Use the extra time with your loved ones, building memories with your children and teaching them of Christ's love, loving a dear friend who needs you in this season, showing kindness to the elderly and other overlooked people, or showering a new pet with all the love in your heart.

How can you allow God to fill the void in your life? How are the Scriptures below helpful?

_____

_____

_____

_____

_____

_____

_____

_____

_____

_____

_____

_____

_____

_____

_____

_____

_____

_____

_____

Digging Deeper with Scripture: Deuteronomy 31:6; Isaiah 43:2–3; 1 Peter 5:7

Loneliness

List prayers and thanksgiving for your child(ren).

List prayers and thanksgiving for yourself and what you have.

Fear

Fear can be the most crippling of emotions for anyone. It can keep you stagnant, hold you back, and stop you from doing everything you want to do for yourself and your child(ren). Most humans fear for a variety of reasons. Fear is part of being normal. I feared—and still fear—making one wrong move that would land us on the street. One Sunday, with only a half tank of gas, I sat in the driveway, dressed in my Sunday finest. There was no extra money for gas; we needed groceries, plus my cell phone bill was due, and there was no money in sight. Too proud to ask for a handout, I drove to church because I had been asked to substitute in the four-year-old classroom—so I wouldn't be fed spiritually, either. But I went anyway.

I put on my fake smile and dropped my son off for kids church. He loved it, so that was a plus. As I walked down the halls of kids church, I silently prayed, "Lord, show me what to do." Apparently, a husband-and-wife team normally taught the four-year-olds, but one of their kids was sick, and the husband had stayed home. The wife was so grateful to have help, and she was happy it was me. As hard as I tried, I could not hide my worry. But I felt the Lord tell me that it was okay to confess my immediate need to her. She wrote me a check for what I needed, right then and there. By the way, she rarely carried her checkbook.

After thanking God and her profusely, I realized that fear could control me, but God could take that control and use it for His good! Our Father desires for us to live in freedom, knowing He will provide.

> *For I am the Lord your God who takes hold of your right hand and says to you, Do not fear; I will help you.*
>
> —Isa. 41:13

Every parent in the world has a fear of failure. Your fear should not rule you, nor should it color your decisions. Let the Lord guide you, protect you, and provide for you. Let these not be mere words on paper, but words to trust in and live by. Letting go of fear and allowing yourself to trust the Lord is hard. It's one of the hardest things I'll ever have to do, but I do so because I know the Lord desires more for me than I could ever desire for myself.

Fear

How can you begin to combat your fears? Are they real fears or lies from the enemy?

_____

_____

_____

_____

_____

_____

_____

_____

_____

_____

_____

_____

_____

_____

_____

_____

_____

_____

_____

Digging Deeper with Scripture: Joshua 1:9; Psalm 23:4, 56:3; Matthew 6:34

List prayers and thanksgiving for your child(ren).

Fear

List prayers and thanksgiving for yourself and what you have.

_____

_____

_____

_____

_____

_____

_____

_____

_____

_____

_____

_____

_____

_____

_____

_____

_____

_____

_____

_____

Anger

Emotions tend to get the best of us, especially anger. Most if not all of us walk around with some level of hurt, which can easily turn into anger—anger over never having enough time, about having to do it all ourselves, or about lacking resources. The list is endless. However, we must not hold on to anger, even if it is justified. Let's face facts: As a working parent, trying to make ends meet, the emotions are intense and real. Nine times out of ten, anger is justified. Being angry is not the sin. Being angry to the point of sinning is wrong in God's eyes. What you do with the anger can be sinful. God wants us to manage it.

> *My dear brothers and sisters, take note of this: Everyone should be quick to listen, slow to speak and slow to become angry.*
>
> —James 1:19

While anger is a natural emotion and a defense mechanism for trying to guard our hearts, we cannot function well under that level of stress. Our bodies are not meant to exist in a heightened state of anger, no matter how justified we are. Our Father wants us to go to Him for everything, in prayer and with thanksgiving. We must trust Him to render justice and mercy in our lives and to those around us. When we make Him the most important part of our lives, we hand Him the anger and let Him take control. We must trust God in all things and leave the justice to Him. Many times, justice will not be served in the world, but that's okay. God's got this.

ANGER

What things enrage you? What can you do to counteract that rage?

Digging Deeper with Scripture: Proverbs 19:11; Psalm 4:4; Ephesians 4:26–27; Colossians 3:8

List prayers and thanksgiving for your child(ren).

Anger

List prayers and thanksgiving for yourself and what you have.

Feeling Like a Failure

We will all feel this burden at some time or another—or even daily. Please know that these feelings come from the enemy who's trying to wreck one of the most precious units in the world—the family. The stronger your unit, the harder the enemy will attack. Just remember that no matter how strong the attack from the enemy, God is stronger and has no rival or equal. Even so, failure is a part of life. How we handle failure is what matters. God has a counterattack for you: His strategies are hope, love, peace, grace, and mercy.

> But those who hope in the LORD *will renew their strength. They will soar on wings like eagles; they will run and not grow weary, they will walk and not be faint.*
> —Isa. 40:31 (emphasis added)

Failures will come. However, if you have hope in the Lord, He can lift you up so that you can be renewed and rejuvenated. The Lord desires to be close to you. Retreat to His Word and talk to Him when you are feeling low. Unlike humans, God is always listening and working all things to your good, even your failures. For a great story of what it looks like when God redeems failure, check out the book of Psalms, many of which were written by King David, who failed miserably many times but was chosen to be part of Jesus's lineage.

Feeling Like a Failure

In what way does knowing that God is a God of peace and mercy alter your feelings of failure? How can you negate the lies with Scripture?

___

Digging Deeper with Scripture: Job 17:15; Psalm 147:11; Jeremiah 29:11

List prayers and thanksgiving for your child(ren).

Feeling Like a Failure

List prayers and thanksgiving for yourself and what you have.

Hate

Harboring hate can become such a habit that we aren't even aware of. It is a deceptive emotion. As justified as we feel, holding on to hate is not what God wants. Even when Jesus was hanging on the cross between two criminals, He pleaded for His Father to forgive those who were hanging beside Him on the cross. Hating your fellow man hurts only you, not the one you hate. Forgiveness is the key to letting go of hate. The world will tell you to hold on to your hate and justify it. However, God wants you to let go of those negative emotions and live in freedom.

> *Jesus said, "Father, forgive them, for they do not know what they are doing." And they divided up his clothes by casting lots.*
>
> —Luke 23:34

God wants us to live free of hate. Letting go of hate is one of the best things you can do for yourself and your children. The opposite of hate is love, forgiveness, and acceptance. Modeling forgiveness for your children is worth the effort. Showing godly love to your fellow man is a vital example for your children. Trust God and allow yourself to build a legacy of love.

What are some ways you can begin to love those you currently hate?

Digging Deeper with Scripture: 1 John 2:9, 3:15; Luke 10:27

List prayers and thanksgiving for your child(ren).

Hate

List prayers and thanksgiving for yourself and what you have.

Being Frustrated

Frustration can become a daily habit for single parents. We can feel helpless and alone as we watch others with spousal support and great families who lend a helping hand. We become most frustrated when circumstances don't improve. Take heart, for the Lord does not want us to live with frustration. This doesn't mean that you will never be frustrated. Even Jesus was frustrated with His disciples and rebuked them. God wants us to be filled with peace, which is the opposite of frustration.

> *Therefore, since we have been justified through faith, we have peace with God through our Lord Jesus Christ.*
> —Rom. 5:1

As a single parent, I encourage you to stop looking at others. Your life with your children is your own. No two families are identical. Often our frustration comes when we compare ourselves to others. Well, guess what: You have no idea what others struggle with. What people present to the world is not always the truth. God is truthful and peaceful. Peace is something we have to work for and pray for. Choose peace and feel your attitude changing.

Being Frustrated

How can having peace affect your daily life? How will having peace decrease your level of frustration?

_____
_____
_____
_____
_____
_____
_____
_____
_____
_____
_____
_____
_____
_____
_____
_____
_____
_____
_____
_____

Digging Deeper with Scripture: 1 Peter 5:7; James 3:18; Colossians 3:15; Philippians 4:7

List prayers and thanksgiving for your child(ren).

BEING FRUSTRATED

List prayers and thanksgiving for yourself and what you have.

_____
_____
_____
_____
_____
_____
_____
_____
_____
_____
_____
_____
_____
_____
_____
_____
_____
_____
_____
_____
_____
_____

Heartache

Heartache is tough. The dictionary defines it as deep anguish or sorrow. As single parents, we will experience heartache from time to time. These feelings can come from the loss of a relationship, the death of a loved one, a situation with your children, or even the loss of material items. It is a normal human emotion. God has experienced heartache over our sins and transgressions. We experience heartache for several reasons, many of which are valid. What we cannot and should not justify is constant heartache.

God is not a God of anguish and sorrow. He is a God of hope and promise. One of the biggest testimonies of heartache and God's faithfulness is in the book of Exodus. All Hebrew boys were to be killed at birth, drowned in the Nile River. But Moses's mother set him afloat down the river where he was found by Pharaoh's daughter. Moses grew up not knowing who his family was. As an adult, he murdered a man and fled Egypt. Later in his life, God called Moses to free the children of Israel and took him back to Egypt to confront Pharaoh, bringing the book of Exodus full circle.

> *Fear not, for I am with you; be not dismayed, for I am your God; I will strengthen you, I will help you, I will uphold you with my righteous right hand.*
>
> —Isa. 41:10 ESV

The sting of loss and the subsequent heartache is never easy. We tend to make light of a very tough subject, but God does not take the subject lightly. He also does not want you to have a hopeless existence filled with heartache. The Bible is full of God's promises and redemption after heartache and loss. I urge you to look beyond your heartache and rely on God. Go to Him in the midst of your heartache. Let Him ease your pain.

Heartache

What are some examples of heartache in the Bible? How did God provide? How does this encourage you?

_____

_____

_____

_____

_____

_____

_____

_____

_____

_____

_____

_____

_____

_____

_____

_____

_____

_____

_____

_____

Digging Deeper with Scripture: Psalm 34:18; Proverbs 14:3; Ecclesiastes 1:18; Romans 9:2

List prayers and thanksgiving for your child(ren).

Heartache

List prayers and thanksgiving for yourself and what you have.

_____
_____
_____
_____
_____
_____
_____
_____
_____
_____
_____
_____
_____
_____
_____
_____
_____
_____
_____

Forgiveness

Forgiveness is not forgetting—but letting go. Forgiveness is for the forgiver, not for the one who wronged us. Forgiveness is godly. Forgiveness is what God gives us each time we confess our sins. Forgiveness is free and freeing.

Knowing the actual meaning of forgiveness is the beginning of walking in freedom and love. As single mothers, we must learn to forgive when we are hurt, neglected, wronged, judged, and mistreated. The Lord is in complete control of the forgiver and the one receiving forgiveness.

> *Get rid of all bitterness, rage and anger, brawling and slander, along with every form of malice. Be kind and compassionate to one another, forgiving each other, just as in Christ God forgave you.*
>
> —Eph. 4:31-32

Forgiving others, especially someone who has hurt you deeply, is not easy. It is a tough decision to change and let go of something you have been holding. However, the Holy Spirit can work within to accomplish forgiveness, which we deem impossible. We have a perfect example of forgiveness in Jesus Christ, who, while He was dying on the cross, cried out for His Father to forgive those who crucified Him. What a powerful depiction of forgiveness!

FORGIVENESS

What do you believe about God forgiving our sins—*all* our sins?

___

Digging Deeper with Scripture: Colossians 3:13; Matthew 6:14–15; 2 Corinthians 5:17

List prayers and thanksgiving for your child(ren).

FORGIVENESS

List prayers and thanksgiving for yourself and what you have.

Pride

Pride is a tough one for any human. On one hand, we can feel unsullied pride (also called *satisfaction*) over a job well-done. On the other hand, we battle a consuming, self-serving pride. The latter is the sinful side of pride. Many times, as single mothers we are too proud to ask for help or acknowledge that we need something. God considers that kind of pride sinful. We are not to be so arrogant—so proud—that we refuse help or turn away, saying, "I can do it myself!"

Pride has kept many non-Christians from having a fruitful relationship with Jesus Christ. Many struggle to admit their sin or confess wrongdoing to God. He desires us to be humble—the opposite of pride—and admit our need so that He can stand in the gap. In your weakness, God can make you strong and receive *all* the glory!

> *Pride goes before destruction and a haughty spirit before a fall. It is better to be of a lowly spirit with the poor than to divide the spoil with the proud.*
> —Prov. 16:18–19 ESV

I urge you to reconsider prideful behavior. Your children are watching. The best way to avoid passing arrogant and prideful behavior on to your children is to display a humble and modest attitude. Humility comes with knowing we can do nothing apart from our Lord and Savior. Many see humility as weakness, but that idea could not be further from the truth. It takes much more courage, resolve, and trust to travel through life with a humble spirit. Moreover, if we're being honest, we would prefer our children to have a humble heart. We must be the model.

PRIDE

Name a time when pride stopped you from asking for help. How did the situation turn out? What humble thoughts can you begin using to replace your prideful thoughts?

_____

_____

_____

_____

_____

_____

_____

_____

_____

_____

_____

_____

_____

_____

_____

_____

_____

Digging Deeper with Scripture: Jeremiah 9:23; Isaiah 23:9; Proverbs 11:2; James 4:6

List prayers and thanksgiving for your child(ren).

Pride

List prayers and thanksgiving for yourself and what you have.

Letting Love In

God can and will create beauty from ashes. When the time is right and when you least expect it, He can restore all that you have lost and more. But you must be ready for it. Many times, when opportunity comes knocking, we're not properly prepared. For years I prayed for my love, Larry. I was specific: I asked God without shame for exactly what I wanted. I prayed, attended Bible studies, met with my mentor one-on-one to discuss my serious sins and work on them. I genuinely worked on myself to be a better Christian and prepared myself to be someone's wife. I felt as if the Lord was preparing me specifically for one man. Then, one day, the Lord dropped that man in my lap—or so it seemed. He was *everything* I had prayed for and more! We had both been praying. We were blissfully happy for the short time God allowed me to have him.

Ask any single momma who is now happily married, and she will tell you that she met the man of her dreams when she least expected to. What she may leave out of her conversation is that she was obedient. She prayed, she was faithful, and she waited for the Lord. She cried out to God alone at night. She did not share her desire to be married with everyone, just a trusted few. Even being ready to let love in takes effort and prayer. There is not a one-size-fits-all approach to dating and letting love in, but there is one Lord, and all our hope is found in Him.

> *Take delight in the* Lord, *and he will give you the desires of your heart.*
> —Ps. 37:4

I cannot guarantee a new love; no one can make that promise. However, trust in the Lord when that amazing man shows up. You will not have to struggle or question his motives. He will shower you and your children with love. He will want to be with *all* of you, not just you alone. He will be a gift from God.

Letting Love In

List prayers and thanksgiving for the love you currently have in your life (i.e., friends and family) and then a prayer for the new love whom you want in your life.

Digging Deeper with Scripture: 1 Timothy 5:14; 1 Corinthians 13:4–7, 16:14; Romans 13:8

List prayers and thanksgiving for your child(ren).

Letting Love In

List prayers and thanksgiving for yourself and what you have.

_____

_____

_____

_____

_____

_____

_____

_____

_____

_____

_____

_____

_____

_____

_____

_____

_____

_____

_____

_____

_____

_____

_____

The Other Parent

The other parent could be the absolute best parent, the worst parent, or the parent no longer with us. But children belong to both parents and have been entrusted to us to care, love, and provide for. God feels strongly about the family unit, so strongly that the Bible begins with Adam and Eve—the first parents. It will be difficult to teach your children to honor someone you no longer like. It can be agonizing to speak of those fathers who are no longer here. And it can be just an absolute gut pinch to those moms whose children's father is alive but just not around. Whatever the circumstances, let your heavenly Father take His place in your life and in the life of your child. Teach your children whom they can lean on in the worst and best of times.

> *Honor your mother and father.*
> —Matt. 19:19

God desires whole families—as whole as they can possibly be. The enemy lurks in the shadows, waiting for the perfect moment to tell you that the other parent is nothing. He says that the other parent will never provide and that no one will ever provide for you and your children—that you will always do it alone. But God's voice is sweet and full of truth. He says, "Come to me . . . and I will give you rest" (Matt. 11:28). He will supply all your needs. There is no need to worry. Who will you choose to listen to?

The Other Parent

List the ways you can be praying to honor your child(ren)'s father more.

_____
_____
_____
_____
_____
_____
_____
_____
_____
_____
_____
_____
_____
_____
_____
_____
_____
_____
_____

List prayers and thanksgiving for your child(ren).

List prayers and thanksgiving for yourself and what you have.

Feeling Safe

Feeling safe sounds odd. But ask any single mom if she feels safe at all times, and her answer will most likely be *no*. I'm not referring to physical safety but emotional safety. That sense of calm and comfort. We do not feel safe when we are getting car repairs alone. We do not feel safe in a room full of married women. We do not feel safe when our children are with their fathers away from us. We do not feel safe around certain people who do not have our best interest at heart. We just do not feel safe. However, God provides safe spaces for us. He shelters us when we are weary and when we need protection. Viewing God as a loving father is a safe place for us even in the middle of chaos.

> The LORD is my Shepherd; I shall not want. He makes me lie down in green pastures. He leads me beside still waters. He restores my soul.
>
> —Ps. 23: 1–3 ESV

God desires to be in a relationship with us and does not desire us to live closed off and alone with no community. Let Him surround you with the right community. In the wrong community, you will not feel safe. Removing yourself from the situation, seeking God, and asking for His protection—this is what we must do when we feel unsafe. God will never hurt you or put you in harm's way. Harm, chaos, and pain come from the enemy. Just as sheep can survive only with the love and guidance of a shepherd, so we can survive only with our Shepherd's protection.

FEELING SAFE

List the ways you can be praying for yourself and your child(ren) to be successful.

List prayers and thanksgiving for your child(ren).

Feeling Safe

List prayers and thanksgiving for yourself and what you have.

_____
_____
_____
_____
_____
_____
_____
_____
_____
_____
_____
_____
_____
_____
_____
_____
_____
_____
_____
_____
_____
_____

Fear of Dying

For you single mothers, your fears of dying and leaving your children are valid. Many if not all single mothers face these fears. They may be irrational or very real depending on your circumstances. When Mitchell was five, I was hospitalized for low potassium. Sounds simple enough, except that potassium is what allows your muscles to function. Lying in the ER thinking about him, I thought my heart would burst with pain. I could not image him growing up without me. I cried out to the Lord, "Not now, God, please, not now!" I knew what God was capable of. I knew I did not serve a God who did not hear me or ignored prayers.

> *For you created my inmost being; you knit me together in my mother's womb. I praise you because I am* fearfully and wonderfully made; your works are wonderful, *I know that full well. . . . Your eyes saw my unformed body.*
> —Ps. 139:13–14, 16a (emphasis added)

The God we serve is omnipresent and omniscient. He knows the exact day of our birth and the exact day of our death. There is nothing in the world we can do about that. He designed us to worship and obey him. He did not give us a spirit of fear. No matter how long we live, we must not live in fear. The fear of dying is something from the enemy. He loathes strong families. Panicking over what may or may not happen to you robs you of living fully present and engaged with your children. Worry cannot add one moment to your life—it robs you of joy! God desires for you to live free from fear and worry and to rest in His goodness.

The Bible says that God has not given us a spirit of fear. What does that mean to you?

_____

_____

_____

_____

_____

_____

_____

_____

_____

_____

_____

_____

_____

_____

_____

_____

_____

_____

Digging Deeper with Scripture: Philippians 4:7; 1 John 4:18; Psalm 34:4, 56:3; Isaiah 41:10

List prayers and thanksgiving for your child(ren).

List prayers and thanksgiving for yourself and what you have.

Personal Matters

Life as a single mom is full of concerns. We feel like we're swimming with an elephant on our back while being chased by a shark. God did not intend for us to struggle like this. We were not supposed to bear the weight of the two-parent role. Take heart: We are not forgotten, nor cast off like a colony of leapers. Our Father, our heavenly Father, is ever present, protecting, and providing for us.

> *Humble yourselves, therefore, under God's mighty hand, that he may lift you up in due time.*
>
> —1 Pet. 5:6

Judgment from Society

Judgment from society will come no matter what. There is nothing we can do about those who choose to judge single mothers and make harsh remarks or treat us a certain way. However, we can control how we respond to each attack and how we treat others. Our heavenly Father expects us to respond to even our enemies in love. He is not asking us to expect love in return, just to give it. When we alter the way we respond, our heart changes, and we are able to withstand the attacks that *will* come.

> *Above all, love each other deeply, because love covers over a multitude of sins.*
> —1 Pet. 4: 8

There will always be judgment. However, there is also forgiveness and free will. As Christians, we can choose between the way the world says to live and the way God has created us to live.

What can you do when you bear the brunt of an unprovoked attack?

Digging Deeper with Scripture: 2 Samuel 7:28; Proverbs 3:5; Psalm 20:7

Judgment from Society

List prayers and thanksgiving for your child(ren).

List prayers and thanksgiving for yourself and what you have.

Friendships

Friendships are the backbone of our lives, especially for single mothers. Some of us are blessed to have help from nearby family, but others are not so fortunate. Therefore, in lieu of family units, our friends become our family. We need, love, and depend on friends just as we need air. It is natural and human to want close relationships with other human beings. God encourages us to live and love in community with one another as the body of Christ.

> *My command is this: Love each other as I have loved you. Greater love has no one than this: to lay down one's life for one's friends. You are my friends if you do what I command.*
> —John 15:12–14

Friendships can make or break us. Are your friendships lifting you up or tearing you down? Are you a support to your friends or a burden? God means for us to live in community with each other to provide support, share one another's difficulties, and worship together.

What kind of people are you choosing to spend time with? Why?

Digging Deeper with Scripture: Job 16:20-21; Proverbs 17:17; Proverbs 18:24; 1 Corinthians 15:33

Friendships

List prayers and thanksgiving for your child(ren).

List prayers and thanksgiving for yourself and what you have.

_____

_____

_____

_____

_____

_____

_____

_____

_____

_____

_____

_____

_____

_____

_____

_____

_____

_____

_____

_____

Taking Care of Yourself

Learning to be mindful to take care of yourself is one of the hardest tasks for a single mother to do. We spend so much time caring for others that we tend to put ourselves dead last. We need to alter that mode of thinking. As the sole caregiver, it is essential for us to be in tiptop shape so that we can care for our children well. If you have ever traveled, I am sure you recall these words from the flight attendant: "In the event of an emergency, oxygen masks will deploy. Please apply your own oxygen mask before helping children and those in need of assistance."

Taking care of ourselves is about much more than just being in good health. God has given us these bodies to honor him. Not taking care of them dishonors God. When you look at it from His point of view, you will make small adjustments in your life to change.

> *Do you not know that your bodies are temples of the Holy Spirit, who is in you, whom you have received from God? You are not your own; you were bought at a price. Therefore honor God with your bodies.*
> —1 Cor. 6:19–20

Taking care of yourself can be as foreign as learning another language. Nevertheless, as children learn, so can adults. The *desire* to learn and grow allows us to evolve into better Christians, parents, family members, and friends. The Bible is a set of instructions. Everything we need is in His Word. He even instructs us to care for our bodies. I am not referring to cosmetic surgery or beauty products, but to healthy foods, exercise, removing toxins and toxic people from our lives, and taking time away to recuperate and recharge.

In what ways can you immediately begin to care for the one body you have been given?

_____

_____

_____

_____

_____

_____

_____

_____

_____

_____

_____

_____

_____

_____

_____

_____

_____

Digging Deeper with Scripture: Proverbs 11:17; 1 Peter 5:7; Romans 12:1

Taking Care of Yourself

List prayers and thanksgiving for your child(ren).

List prayers and thanksgiving for yourself and what you have.

Realizing What Is Important

Realizing what's important as a single mother is an aha moment. We wear a variety of hats, many of them simultaneously and for extended periods. When everything seems important, it's difficult to differentiate what is *actually* important. I use a saying I heard from an older single mother with grown, professional, well-adjusted children. When I asked her how she managed it all and determined what was and wasn't important, she looked at me with the straightest face and answered, "I ask myself, 'Will it matter in five minutes, five days, or five years?' If the answer is no, the item, idea, or situation is not important." The statement was short but so freeing. When things get hectic, as they will, stop and ask that question. God did not design us to live in chaos and confusion. He designed us to live in harmony with Him and with each other.

> *If any of you lacks wisdom, you should ask God, who gives generously to all without finding fault, and it will be given to you.*
>
> —James 1:5

We could spin our wheels trying to get it all done, but in the end, all we will be is more anxious and stressed than we were before. There will come a time when you realize that you cannot do it all. But there is a way to do the most important things you need done. Going to God in prayer is key. Your relationship with Him *is* the most important thing in your life. Everything else is secondary.

How can you use the Scripture below to help you prioritize your life?

Digging Deeper with Scripture: Proverbs 1:7, 18:15; 2 Timothy 2:7

Realizing What Is Important

List prayers and thanksgiving for your child(ren).

List prayers and thanksgiving for yourself and what you have.

Death and Dying

Losing loved ones is a normal part of life, but it doesn't feel normal. It's overwhelming and consuming. Nothing seems to help at first. You waffle through the stages of grief like an emotional teenager. It is by far the hardest disappointment you'll ever have to deal with. It doesn't seem fair that someone so special is taken from you. You have so many questions: Why me? Why now? Don't I have enough on my plate? Lord Jesus, please!

You agonize over what you could have done differently. You think about the last conversation you had with the person. The constant spinning of your mind is only stopped by the flow of tears. They seem constant. Then you sit and stare, so numb you think you'll never move again. To top everything off, during your grief, you can't stop being Mom. Your children still need and want you. Life for them may continue to be very normal while your foundation is crumbling.

This is the moment when you stop trying to do it all. Let others help and come in. Ask people if they can take your children for a night or two. There is no manual for how you will deal with grief. Don't try to hide your grief from your children. When I lost my love, I would try to cook and end up standing in the kitchen crying. Letting go of fear and allowing yourself to trust the Lord is hard. My son would come in and look so defeated. I had to start telling him there was nothing he could do. I had to keep telling him, "Mommy is just sad. I am going to cry, and you will see my tears, and it is okay. We will be okay." God will wait for the time when you are ready, when you can do more than just breathe, when you can hear and comprehend Scripture again. He is waiting. Let Him in. Allow the Lord to be your comfort and the way forward. There is no magic answer. Death hurts in a way that I am not able to put into words, but God knows and understands it all.

Blessed are those who mourn, for they will be comforted.
—Matt. 5:4

God is always there. He will wait for the day when you are ready to stand again, and He will anchor you. You will never be the same. You will never view death the same way again. Your ability to be compassionate toward another will be magnified. Nothing the Lord does comes back void. You will survive this, but it will take time.

Death and Dying

How can you specifically pray about your loss? Have you considered asking others for specific prayers?

_____

_____

_____

_____

_____

_____

_____

_____

_____

_____

_____

_____

_____

_____

_____

_____

_____

_____

Digging Deeper with Scripture: Psalm 34:18; 2 Corinthians 1:3–4; Revelation 21:4; John 14:27

List prayers and thanksgiving for your child(ren).

Death and Dying

List prayers and thanksgiving for yourself and what you have.

Dating

Dating as a single mother should come with hazmat certifications. When you're ready to dive into the dating pool again, you will need God more than ever. The world of dating has changed in the last half century, but God's Word is true. It is trustworthy. God is working all things for His glory, including but not limited to your dating life. The Bible does not discuss dating, but it does refer to courtship. Biblical courtship depicts a man and woman prayerfully and purposefully determining if marriage is in God's plan for them. Date in pursuit of marriage and remember that we must not entertain unbelievers.

> *Do not be unequally yoked with unbelievers. For what partnership has righteousness with lawlessness? Or what fellowship has light with darkness? What accord has Christ with Belial? Or what portion does a believer share with an unbeliever?*
> —2 Cor. 6:14–15 ESV

Dating as a Christian and a single mother presents its own unique set of challenges. Because we have children, many of us have hard and fast rules regarding dating and the type of men we will and will not allow in our life. God grants us the gift of discernment for occasions such as this. While discernment may lengthen the wait for a mate, it will be well worth it. Waiting gives you time to spend on yourself, your walk, your prayer life, and your time with the Lord.

The world will tell you lies. Search your heart and ask your heavenly Father what is true. I prayed for Larry, my love, for seven years. I had a list of items I prayed over and wanted in a husband for myself and a father for Mitchell. About a year into dating him, I pulled out that list and compared it to the man. He had 99 out of 100 things on the list, and the one thing He did not have did not matter. I am grateful that God showed me that he does answer prayer.

Dating

How does your dating life look now? Are you honoring God in your relationships?

___

Digging Deeper with Scripture: 2 Corinthians 6:14; Ecclesiastes 4:9–12; 1 Thessalonians 5:11

List prayers and thanksgiving for your child(ren).

DATING

List prayers and thanksgiving for yourself and what you have.

Blame Game

The blame game is extremely easy to play for all parents. We blame the world for our not having enough money, but have we prepared and saved? We blame schools for not teaching our children, but aren't we our children's *primary* teacher? We blame the other parent for what they are or are not doing, but all we can control is ourselves. The list is endless. However, God is a God of mercy and grace. Grace is God's undeserved favor. Blaming is ungodly. Taking responsibility for your actions is not only the right thing to do; it is right in the eyes of God.

I blamed my son's father for not supporting us for years. One day, I felt convicted by the Holy Spirit and just stopped. I told him I would support and provide for our child, and I would never ask him for another dime. I have not spoken to him about money since, but God changed his attitude. He started paying child support and visiting more often a few years after I stopped speaking to him about monetary support. There is power in prayer and power in holding your tongue.

> *Whoever conceals his transgressions will not prosper, but he who confesses and forsakes them will obtain mercy.*
> —Prov. 28:13 ESV

Taking responsibility is not a public display for the world to see, but rather a private interaction with and confession to our Father. We do not need the world to know we are doing the right thing or taking responsibility. I urge you not to be concerned with what the world thinks. God is watching everyone. Be sure you are taking responsibility for your own actions. If you have played the blame game and are wrong, take your confessions to Him. He will forgive even the worst offenses.

Blame Game

What is the definition of grace? How can you show grace to yourself?

_____
_____
_____
_____
_____
_____
_____
_____
_____
_____
_____
_____
_____
_____
_____
_____
_____

Digging Deeper with Scripture: Hebrews 4:16; 2 Corinthians 12:8–9; Ephesians 4:7, 2:8–9

List prayers and thanksgiving for your child(ren).

Blame Game

List prayers and thanksgiving for yourself and what you have.

Ashamed of Our Failures

Being ashamed of our failures and shortcomings can be a horrible constant in a single mother's life. We feel like failures if our children aren't doing well in school, if we can't keep the house as clean as we would like it, or if we aren't able to put amazing five-course meals on the table after work. We feel like failures when we can't be in two places at once, and there isn't enough money. For many reasons, we feel as if we come up short. Rest assured: God's faithfulness is bigger than any failure that we feel. He doesn't make mistakes. He is working all things to His glory so that even your failures will one day be triumph.

> *Because of the LORD's great love we are not consumed, for his compassions never fail. They are new every morning; great is your faithfulness.*
>
> —Lam. 3:22–23

The enemy will put lies in your head. The enemy will call you a failure for being a single mother and not providing in the same way two-parent homes provide. God has not called us to wallow in self-pity or believe the lies or spiral down into a web of depression. His desire is for your worship. He instructs all parents to raise children in a loving home with God as the focus. With God on our side, we need not be ashamed of anything. He is a God of second chances; we can begin again—today.

I used to be so ashamed that I lacked a college degree. I tried to go back to college several times, but my heart was not in it. Finally, after much prayer, confessing to God what I felt was a failure on my part, he changed my heart and began to show me that my gifts had nothing to do with a degree.

Ashamed of Our Failures

What can you do to refocus your attention on your successes? How can you show yourself grace and mercy?

_____

Digging Deeper with Scripture: Isaiah 40:13; 2 Corinthians 4:9; 2 Timothy 1:7

List prayers and thanksgiving for your child(ren).

Ashamed of Our Failures

List prayers and thanksgiving for yourself and what you have.

Guilt and Shame

As single mothers, we feel guilt and shame that our kids have only one parent, that they have less than what other children have, that they are growing up without a father or father figure, and that they'll have to deal with the results of our messes. But the truth is that believers have no claim to guilt or shame. You need to know, understand, comprehend, and truly *get* the fact that Jesus died on the cross for our sins, *all* our sins—not just a few. As He was dying, the thief next to Him asked for forgiveness and a place in paradise, and Jesus forgave him *immediately and eternally.*

Once you understand that your sins are forgiven, there is no need to feel guilt and shame over anything you have done. Now, there might be consequences for your actions, but the shame needs to be left at the door. The blood of the lamb covers you! However, the guilt and shame that we all feel as single mothers is strong, and for some of us, it is a constant. But it is not from God. It comes from the enemy who designed it to keep you stagnant and depressed. God's design for you is to live in harmony with Him and to feel His hope and His love.

> *If we confess our sins, he is faithful and just to forgive us our sins and to cleanse us from all unrighteousness.*
> —1 John 1:9 ESV

Please know that all mothers, single and married, feel aspects of "mom guilt"—those lies from the enemy saying that we should be ashamed for not being perfect. While the enemy is the father of lies, our God is the author of truth. The Bible is full of His truth. Get still and listen for the small steady voice at the back of the room telling you that you are loved and that you belong to God. I pray that you hear that message over all the noisy lies in the world. God wants you to know that He loves you. Go to Him and ask for help. He will equip you.

Guilt and Shame

What are some biblical ways we can begin to forgive ourselves?

Digging Deeper with Scripture: Isaiah 38:17; Psalm 51:1–2, 103:2; Romans 5:1

List prayers and thanksgiving for your child(ren).

Guilt and Shame

List prayers and thanksgiving for yourself and what you have.

_____
_____
_____
_____
_____
_____
_____
_____
_____
_____
_____
_____
_____
_____
_____
_____
_____
_____
_____
_____
_____
_____

Self-Worth

Self-worth refers to the value that we feel we are worth. Many of us do not have a high opinion of ourselves. Because single mothers already feel alone and overwhelmed, they often feel unvalued. Perhaps no one has ever told you what you are worth, or worse yet, perhaps someone has told you that you are worth*less*! But you are far from worthless. While the Bible does not address self-worth, it does refer to your image. Your Heavenly Father sees you as a daughter of the King. You were made in His image, and neither He nor His designs are *ever* flawed. Our self-worth is in His power, His majesty, His strength, His righteousness, and His Word.

> *But the LORD said to Samuel, "Do not consider his appearance or his height, for I have rejected him. The LORD does not look at the things people look at. People look at the outward appearance, but the LORD looks at the heart."*
> —1 Sam. 16:7

The world will tell you that your self-worth should be wrapped up in your home, car, money, job, or outward beauty. These things are far from the truth. The world will tell you that good people finish last. The world will tell you since you are an unmarried mother, you are not worthy of love, security, or blessings. These are all lies from the enemy. One Samuel 16:7 points out that while man looks at the outside, the Lord is looking at the inside. The Holy Spirit resides in you. You are a beautiful, living, breathing extension of God the Father. You are a Daughter of the King, and you are raising His heirs—a high and holy calling!

Self-Worth

Where does your self-worth come from? Which Scripture verses below can you repeat to combat the negative thoughts when they come?

_____

_____

_____

_____

_____

_____

_____

_____

_____

_____

_____

_____

_____

_____

_____

_____

_____

_____

Digging Deeper with Scripture: Psalm 139:13–14; Proverbs 31:25; Romans 5:8, 12:3

List prayers and thanksgiving for your child(ren).

Self-Worth

List prayers and thanksgiving for yourself and what you have.

___

Difficult Family

The hard part about family is that you did not choose them, and they did not choose you. However, God did choose all of you for each other. God knew what you would need years down the line. He knew the lessons you had to learn before you were born. It's easy to think that some people have a picture-perfect family while yours seems less than stellar. The truth is that we all struggle at some point with family relationships. So, what do we do about it? How do we change those around us? The answer is this: we cannot change anyone but ourselves. We need to examine how we choose to respond to those around us. Can we make a heart change, and are we ready to? Do you feel the pain is too great to overcome? I had a terrible relationship with my father. I longed for him to be something he wasn't capable of. It took me years to finally forgive him, even though he never apologized to me. He passed away, and I made peace with it all. Sadly, he did not truly know me, and he saw my son only twice but never held him.

> *Have I not commanded you? Be strong and courageous. Do not be afraid; do not be discouraged, for the LORD your God will be with you wherever you go.*
> —Josh. 1:9

Dealing with family is so personal but so important for protecting the family unit. Some of the hurt and issues go so deep that they hurt us to the core. In these moments, we must turn to the Lord to change hearts and to make a way out of no way. We Christians are called to love others, even family.

Difficult Family

List prayers and thanksgiving for your family, even the difficult ones.

_____

_____

_____

_____

_____

_____

_____

_____

_____

_____

_____

_____

_____

_____

_____

_____

_____

_____

_____

_____

Digging Deeper with Scripture: Matthew 10:34–36; Ephesians 6:1–3; 1 Timothy 5:2

List prayers and thanksgiving for your child(ren).

Difficult Family

List prayers and thanksgiving for you and what you have.

Not Having Enough

Many money managers and religious people speak of a scarcity mindset—that is always feeling as if you will never have enough food, money, emotions, or whatever idea you might fixate on. It is easy to trap yourself into thinking that you will never have enough, but that trap is a lie from the enemy.

Enough means different things to different people. I have friends who ski every year. They have a place in Utah and seem to have amazing vacations. My love was a country boy who grew up in a small town outside of Fort Worth. The first time he took me home, he was so happy to show me pastures where he'd played as a young boy, fishing holes, and the wild hogs. I absolutely loved being in his truck, riding through the countryside and hearing about his childhood. To anyone looking on and comparing the two, it would appear that the ski vacations were much better than the days in the country. However, my love and I both loved being in the country. It became my retreat. Being with him at his father's place and the lake was enough. I could have sat with him on that front porch for the rest of my life. Having enough means different things to different people. We need to reorient our minds on God instead of this world. When you reorient and refocus on God, the idea of enough will begin to change. God is enough!

> *Trust in the L*ORD *with all your heart and lean not on your own understanding; in all your ways submit to him, and he will make your paths straight.*
>
> —Prov. 3:5–6

If you live by a scarcity mindset, there will never be enough. However, if you turn to Christ and become His follower, God will supply all your needs according to His glorious riches.

NOT HAVING ENOUGH

List the things in your life you are grateful for that have no monetary value.

_____

_____

_____

_____

_____

_____

_____

_____

_____

_____

_____

_____

_____

_____

_____

_____

_____

_____

_____

Digging Deeper with Scripture: Psalm 78:24; Proverbs 3:5; Romans 12:2; Luke 16:10; Hebrews 11:1

List prayers and thanksgiving for your child(ren).

Not Having Enough

List prayers and thanksgiving for yourself and what you have.

_____

_____

_____

_____

_____

_____

_____

_____

_____

_____

_____

_____

_____

_____

_____

_____

_____

_____

_____

_____

Legal Battles

Legal battles over money and custody will happen. They are a sad part of human culture. As Christians, we are called to live in unity, love our neighbor, and to turn the other cheek. However, the idea behind court battles is to take from another party, to have a spirit of adversity, to declare war with no room for reconciliation. While the Bible does not speak about child custody or alimony, there are skilled Christians in the legal system who are guided by the Holy Spirit.

> *For the L<small>ORD</small> gives wisdom; from his mouth come knowledge and understanding; he stores up sound wisdom for the upright, he is a shield to those who walk in integrity.*
> —Prov. 2:6–7 ESV

I urge all single mothers to pray before pursuing a legal battle. The battles are long and expensive, and many times the outcome is not what we expect. Make sure your motives are clear and godly. Ungodly motives are sinful, and sin will take you farther than you ever wanted to go and leave you there much longer than you can imagine. Please carefully consider your battle.

Legal Battles

What does it look like for you to pray for direction and guidance?

Digging Deeper with Scripture: Isaiah 50:8–11; Matthew 5:25–26, 18:21–22

List prayers and thanksgiving for your child(ren).

Legal Battles

List prayers and thanksgiving for yourself and what you have.

Practical Matters

Most of the time, we think we have life under control, don't we? That is the exact lie the enemy wants us to believe. The enemy isn't some idiot thug waiting to beat you up. Oh no, the enemy is cool, calm, and collected. His way is to deceive and lie, to trip us up and get us hung up on wrong thinking. Let's face it: the practical matters are small—and we don't think we need God for the small things. The enemy is smart—smarter than we think, but he will never be equal to God! Trust God with everything! He wants to be in all our details.

> *The LORD is my strength and my song; he has become my salvation.*
>
> —Psalm 118:14 ESV

Making Ends Meet

Making ends meet is the constant challenge for a single mother, even with promotions and raises. We feel overwhelmed with financial responsibility no matter what. We question every move and every penny. If we budget, somehow the money disappears on an emergency or some extra need. There never seems to be enough, and the endless mental questions we ask ourselves are maddening. Are we saving enough? What if there is an emergency? Who pays for college? Can we afford summer camp? But this kind of destructive thinking is not what God has designed for us. We were designed to worship him, and he will care for us and our every need.

> *And my God will meet all your needs according to the riches of his glory in Christ Jesus.*
> —Phil. 4:19

We work to live, not live to work. While making ends meet is a constant goal, there are seasons when working more is not an option. The season when your children are young is meant for you to pour into your children. Other seasons present opportunities for you to work more and save. Pray to discern the difference. Listen to your Creator to know which season you are in. Money is important, but it is not everything. Your relationship with God is most important; everything else hinges on that.

What specific prayers can you use to replace all the endless questions that bombard your thoughts? What are three steps you can take immediately to better manage your money?

___

Digging Deeper with Scripture: Proverbs 22:7; Ecclesiastes 5:10; Matthew 6:21

Making Ends Meet

List prayers and thanksgiving for your child(ren).

List prayers and thanksgiving for yourself and what you have.

Balancing It All

Struggling with balance is tough for any mother. For the single working mother, achieving balance seems impossible. Being pulled in more directions than can be counted will eventually limit our ability to be effective. We cannot stop or drop the items we need to balance. Those items are normally work, school, children, cooking, cleaning, and quality time with the kiddos. So how does a single mother juggle it all and not fall into a deep depression when nothing comes to fruition? We pray often. Balance begins with God first. If God is not first, everything falls apart—fast!

> *But all things should be done decently and in order.*
> —1 Cor. 14:40 ESV

Know that all humans struggle for balance. You are never alone. Going to the Creator with your prayers and your pain is what He wants. Let Him take the struggle from you. Let God balance what needs to be balanced so that you can focus on your children. You can't fathom the sweetness that comes from trusting God until you practice trusting Him.

What changes will you make in your prayers to gain guidance from God?

Digging Deeper with Scripture: Psalm 32:8, 25:5–9; John 16:13; Matthew 7:7–11

Balancing It All

List prayers and thanksgiving for your child(ren).

List prayers and thanksgiving for yourself and what you have.

Discipline

Discipline and love are the backbone of childrearing. The Bible is clear on discipline. It is also clear on disciplining fairly and explaining the discipline so children learn from it. Parents must discipline out of love for their children and ultimately for God. It is much easier to do nothing and let children run wild than it is to rebuke them and make corrections. Discipline takes time, energy, and effort. God clearly told us how to live, and He promises discipline if we stray. He loves us too much to leave us to our own devices.

> *And have you completely forgotten this word of encouragement that addresses you as a father addresses his son? It says, "My son, do not make light of the Lord's discipline, and do not lose heart when he rebukes you, because the Lord disciplines the one he loves, and he chastens everyone he accepts as his son."*
> —Heb. 12:5–6

Being the only parent places single mothers in a role originally meant for two parents. Being the loving parent and disciplinarian is a tough combination. You want to be the loving mother, and in the same breath, you want your children to obey and be respectful, but you feel guilty punishing them. God requires us to be obedient and to raise obedient children; therefore, teaching and disciplining must be part of your childrearing. The results are worth the effort.

Did you know God calls us to discipline? Why is discipline important? How can you begin to incorporate it into the lives of your child(ren)?

Digging Deeper with Scripture: Proverbs 12:1, 13:24, 22:6; Ephesians 6:4

Discipline

List prayers and thanksgiving for your child(ren).

List prayers and thanksgiving for yourself and what you have.

Sex

Sex is a gift from God intended for a husband and wife. It is the physical representation of two souls joining together emotionally and spiritually. I'm in no way trying to make single mothers feel horrible or stressed that they will never have physical relations. I am merely explaining what God intended sex to be.

Let me break that down. Sex is meant to be the most intimate union of two souls who are united in Christ, love, and marriage. Sex is *not* a fleeting physical thing that just happens, nor is it the beginning or foundation of a relationship. Sex is meant to deepen the marital relationship by connecting a man and a woman in a physical way *after* they have connected spiritually and emotionally. This is what we should strive for and work toward. Anything less will always feel and be less!

> *The* Lord *God said, "It is not good for the man to be alone. I will make a helper suitable for him."*
>
> —Gen. 2:18

Sex is a difficult subject inside and outside the Bible. Many believe that what was written centuries ago does not apply today, but God meant His Word to be for all time. In no way, shape, or form does this truth mean that you will be single all your life. It means that we need to do things in the way and order God intended and praise Him for delivering us from sin.

How can you immediately honor God with your body? Did you know you can pray for God to remove sinful thoughts and desires?

Digging Deeper with Scripture: Acts 15:19–20; 1 Thessalonians 4:3–5; 1 Corinthians 7:8–9

Sex

List prayers and thanksgiving for your child(ren).

List prayers and thanksgiving for yourself and what you have.

Mentors for Your Children

God did not mean for us to be everything to our children. They need family and friends to live in community with one another—as God intended for all of us. In a perfect world, children should be surrounded by godly adults, church members, teachers, and neighbors. Even in two-parent homes, where children should have the benefit of family, friends, and community from both sides, they do not. Single-parent homes are no different. In fact, our children need it even more.

Mentorship is a recurring theme in the Bible. Moses mentored Joshua, Jesus mentored his disciples, and Paul mentored Timothy. The most significant relationships in my life have been mentorships with men and women in and out of my family. My son has several close relationships with family members and a fantastic mentor in his youth group.

Give instruction to a wise man, and he will be still wiser,
Teach a righteous man and he will increase his learning.
—Prov. 9:9 ESV

I encourage you not to dismiss mentorship. Our children cannot get everything from us. They need and will benefit from other loving adult relationships. If you are unable to connect with a church family, I encourage you to seek out qualified adults who are willing and able to pour into your children. There are many organizations with stellar mentorship programs for young girls and boys. My son's mentorship from Big Brothers Big Sisters of Houston makes my heart sing. Due to COVID-19, they cannot meet personally, but they spend an hour on the phone each month and look forward to their catch-up time.

Why are mentors important for adults? Why are they important for children?

Digging Deeper with Scripture: 2 Timothy 2:2; Proverbs 22:6, 27:17; Matthew 28:19–20

List prayers and thanksgiving for your child(ren).

List prayers and thanksgiving for yourself and what you have.

Our Mentors

Many of us have a few people we turn to for advice, a shoulder to cry on, prayer, help raising our children, and support for each season of life's challenges. Some seasons are much harder than others. In the incredibly hard seasons, a person may step up unexpectedly and give you exactly what you need.

About a year before I lost my love, I met Liv at work. She sat in front of me and told her painful story of losing her sister and getting a divorce. I listened with an empathy I had never known before. She looked at me and said, "I have no idea why I am telling you all of this." I lost my love a year later, and when I felt his spirit had left his body, I knew in that instant why Liv had come into my life. I leaned on her heavily the first couple of weeks, and she let me. She would come to my desk and say, "Let's take a walk." She helped me find my footing and made me realize grief was not something I could run from—I needed professional help to get through it. She was and is a beautiful soul in my life. We still talk, although not nearly as much as we did.

Most times when the crisis is over, the supportive folks simply fade into the background. These are our mentors, whether you recognize them for what they are or not is irrelevant. We all need a person to speak truth into our lives, to cover us in prayer, and be that moral compass for us. In different seasons, we need different mentors.

> *Likewise, teach the older women to be reverent in the way they live, not to be slanderers or addicted to much wine, but to teach what is good.*
>
> —Titus 2:3

Mentors are not always friends, but some become that. Mentors provide instruction in certain areas; they are not meant to stay in your life forever. They are guides in this world during certain seasons of your life. Accept what they are and the lessons they teach. The Bible speaks of older women teaching the younger women, and there is a beautiful example of a godly wife in Proverbs 31, the wise wife who teaches with kindness. These are the biblical examples of what a mentor can look like in our lives.

Our Mentors

How can you be praying for a specific mentor to help you with a trouble spot in your life?

Digging Deeper with Scripture: 1 Timothy 4:14; 1 Peter 4:10; Proverbs 23:12

List prayers and thanksgiving for your child(ren).

Our Mentors

List prayers and thanksgiving for yourself and what you have.

_____

_____

_____

_____

_____

_____

_____

_____

_____

_____

_____

_____

_____

_____

_____

_____

_____

_____

_____

_____

_____

_____

Being Deceived

Being deceived is one of the most sickening feelings on the planet. There are people in this world who actively strive to deceive you: the slimy salesman, the mechanic who knows he can price-gouge, or the so-called friend using you to gain vital information. These are the folks who do not share your values or possibly even your faith. Whatever they do, or have done, is not your issue. It is how you handle the information and situation that will set you apart. It is your faith in Jesus Christ as your personal Lord and Savior that will allow you to rise above the pettiness of others and move forward in life.

> *The heart is deceitful above all things and beyond cure. Who can understand it?*
>
> —Jer. 17:9

Being deceived just flat-out hurts; it stabs a place deep in your heart. The hardest part about deceit is that it makes you feel like a fool for being fooled. Remember that only God knows the hearts of men. Our God is not a liar or cheat. He is loving, fair, and honest. Let the Lord take care of those who deceive. It is not our job to figure out why people do what they do. We can only learn and grow from it.

Being Deceived

List some ways you have been deceived. Then list some actions you can take to not let that happen again. What responsibility do you take for the deceit? How can you show yourself grace?

_____

_____

_____

_____

_____

_____

_____

_____

_____

_____

_____

_____

_____

_____

_____

_____

Digging Deeper with Scripture: Ephesians 4:22; 2 John 7; James 1:26

List prayers and thanksgiving for your child(ren).

Being Deceived

List prayers and thanksgiving for yourself and what you have.

Making Hard Decisions

Sometimes, life requires hard decisions. Many times, single moms are faced with choosing between a rock and a hard place. Then we second-guess the decision, anguish over it, and many times lose sleep. Have we done the right thing? Will this turn out okay? What happens if it doesn't go well? Where do I go when I am all tapped out? Deciding is tough but with intense prayer and the Lord to steady you, you can do this. We all can.

Making one good yet hard decision can change the trajectory of your life. I owned a small business before my son was born, and I wanted to continue it afterward. But I had no funds, no more retirement, and no savings. Looking back, it was one of the toughest decisions I ever made. Mitchell was a baby. I was his only support, and I was down to almost nothing, but I did know how to interview, source, and place nannies. It was a skill I had honed for years without knowing it, but God knew. I took $30 and made 25 beautiful postcards advertising my agency; then I sent them to three streets that I knew from my nannying days. One of the postcards landed on the doorstep of a large mom-to-be shop, and they asked me to become their nanny agency. I was able to make money for them in a matter of days.

No matter what your station in life, you will have difficult decisions to make. Pray often and ask for guidance. That is all I am asking you to do: Trust God, not man. Making a sound decision with God as your guide is a game changer.

> *Whoever gives heed to instruction prospers, and blessed is the one who trusts in the Lord.*
>
> —Prov. 16:20

Making Hard Decisions

When you are faced with making hard choices, tackle the most difficult decision first. Everything won't always fall into place, but once the largest decision is off your plate, you will be in a much better state to make the smaller decisions. Remember that God created the heavens and the earth before he created man. Do the hardest thing first.

What difficult decisions do you face today? What is the most difficult decision? How do you feel after having made the most difficult choice first?

_____

_____

_____

_____

_____

_____

_____

_____

_____

_____

_____

_____

_____

_____

_____

_____

_____

Digging Deeper with Scripture: Joel 3:14; Psalm 22:5, 26:1, 112:7

MAKING HARD DECISIONS

List prayers and thanksgiving for your child(ren).

List prayers and thanksgiving for yourself and what you have.

Time Management

Managing time is one of the hardest tasks for any single mother. Most days, people are pulling from both ends. Everyone needs something right now, and there is only you to do it! Your children, family, boss, ministry, friends—all need time that you do not have. You feel as if you can't check anything off your to-do list. The conflict is never-ending. But the Lord knows what and who is important at certain stages in your life. And there is a time and a place for most things you want to do. Learning to recognize and prioritize the necessary things in your life is a challenge. The world will give you many ways to manage your time:

1. Set goals that are achievable and measurable.
2. Set a time limit to complete a task.
3. Organize yourself. Remove nonessential tasks/activities.
4. Plan.

This list looks great and has helped many people, and it may possibly help you. However, the Bible has set rules on how to manage our time, and the first task is to seek God.

> *Be very careful, then, how you live—not as unwise but as wise, making the most of every opportunity, because the days are evil. Therefore do not be foolish, but understand what the Lord's will is.*
>
> —Eph. 5:15–17

After I lost my love, it was impossible for me to manage my time well. I was so lost, and my inability to prioritize caused me even more stress. Once I began to remember whose I was, I once again gave God my time first. I could feel the shift. Time management is difficult when it is just you; there are so many things pulling at you, and everything seems to need your attention all at once. But seeking God first clears your mind, allowing the Spirit to speak to you and to guide you. Be sure to seek God first. It really is all you need.

Time Management

List prayers and thanksgiving for all you have going on, even the hard stuff. How can you put God first in your life?

_____

_____

_____

_____

_____

_____

_____

_____

_____

_____

_____

_____

_____

_____

_____

_____

_____

_____

_____

_____

_____

Digging Deeper with Scripture: Proverbs 16:9; Luke 14:28; Psalm 90:12; John 16:13

List prayers and thanksgiving for your child(ren).

Time Management

List prayers and thanksgiving for yourself and what you have.

Exercise

Remember that Bible verse that says your body is a temple? Yeah . . . that one.

Believe it. It is there for a reason. Your body is not meant to run on black coffee, three hours of sleep, and leftovers from your kid's lunch. No, ma'am! You will run yourself into the ground! And for what? If you're not around, who will care for your children? If your children are running you into the ground, teach them not to. Set boundaries. Now, you will still have the occasional long night, the hard seasons when you do not sleep or do not get as much exercise as you want. That is not what I am referring to. I am speaking to the moms who specifically ignore their bodies and opt to take care of everyone else except themselves. Guess what? Exercise is fuel. Exercise is life-giving, and your body needs it. Man was not made to sit in one spot and not move. If you do not care for your body, your body will start breaking down prematurely. And then what?

> *Do you not know that your bodies are temples of the Holy Spirit, who is in you, whom you have received from God? You are not your own, you were bought at a price. Therefore, honor God with your bodies.*
>
> —1 Cor. 6:19–20

I went for years without taking care of myself, foolishly thinking that getting up early was too much like punishment for me. Here I am years later with my eyes consistently popping open before 6:30 a.m., giving me time alone to be with the Lord and to exercise. God always provides. Please do not think you don't have time for 15 minutes of exercise a day for some stretching. You will never regret a day you spend taking care of yourself and your body.

Exercise

How can you be praying for better health, and what items can you take off your to-do list to get 15 minutes alone to exercise?

_____

_____

_____

_____

_____

_____

_____

_____

_____

_____

_____

_____

_____

_____

_____

_____

_____

_____

_____

_____

Digging Deeper with Scripture: 1 Timothy 4:8; 1 Corinthians 9:24; Proverbs 10:4

List prayers and thanksgiving for your child(ren).

Exercise

List prayers and thanksgiving for yourself and what you have.

Matters of Faith

Faith is personal. At the heart of Christianity is the truth that Jesus Christ died for our sins. There is no amount of work we can do on our own to get right with God. Simply put, the good news is that Jesus came to save us. If you have never trusted the Lord, it is not too late. God is waiting on you. He desires a relationship with you, His adopted daughter. Your faith can and will start as small as an apple seed, but you can study, worship, and learn. That seed of faith will grow and yield fruit you never even dreamed of. This is the legacy you want to leave for your children.

> *Consequently, faith comes from hearing the message, and the message is heard through the word about Christ.*
> —Rom. 10:17

Lies of the Enemy

Lies of the enemy are deceptive and can lead you down a path of self-loathing and doubt. God is full of goodness and mercy. He does not want you to believe the lies in your head: that you are stupid, that you are not a good parent, that your children will be scarred, that you will never marry, that you are worthless. The list is endless, and the temptation to believe the lies is great. I urge you to replace the lies with truth and let the truth set you free.

> *To the Jews who had believed in him, Jesus said, "If you hold to my teaching, you are really my disciples. Then you will know the truth, and the truth will set you free."*
> —John 8:31–32

You are a child of God, and He has designed you in His image. Lies can trick us and send us spiraling down into despair. That is what the enemy wants. The enemy wants you to be a slave to deception, fear, and worry. However, you do not belong to the enemy. If you have placed your faith in Jesus Christ, you are a child of God. God is the King who reigns supreme, and as His child, you are royalty. Conduct yourselves accordingly!

What truth from Scripture can you use to replace the lies in your head? How can you identify the lies?

Digging Deeper with Scripture: 2 Samuel 7:28; Psalm 20:7; Proverbs 3:5

List prayers and thanksgiving for your child(ren).

List prayers and thanksgiving for yourself and what you have.

Unanswered Prayers

Unanswered prayers hurt. Why wouldn't God grant our every prayer? We are single, after all, and already dealing with so much. Why would He not give us what we want? The answer is simple: what we want and pray for may not be what we need or what he desires for our lives. We have our own agendas and want what we want when we want it. However, God has an agenda as well, and it is for our good.

> *What causes fights and quarrels among you? Don't they come from your desires that battle within you? You desire but do not have, so you kill. You covet but you cannot get what you want, so you quarrel and fight. You do not have because you do not ask God. When you ask, you do not receive, because you ask with wrong motives, that you may spend what you get on your pleasures.*
>
> —James 4:1–3

The world will tell of the harshness of God. His Word will tell you of His goodness. He is our Father. He is a protector and provider. We tell our children no to keep them from harm and to protect them. God loves you more than you know. He loves you enough to say no. Perhaps what you perceive as unanswered prayer is his answering with what you would consider a surprising twist. Aren't you thrilled God is in control?

What have you been praying for that may not be God's will but your own? What can you be praying for that would be more in line with God's will for your life and the lives of your children?

___

Digging Deeper with Scripture: Psalm 27:14, 130:5; Isaiah 30:18; James 5:7–8

Unanswered Prayers

List prayers and thanksgiving for your child(ren).

List prayers and thanksgiving for yourself and what you have.

How to Begin/Revive a Prayer Life

How do you begin a prayer life or revive one? Taking one step at a time is the key. God desires your worship and welcomes it. There are so many ways to praise Him: through song, thanksgiving, praise and worship, reading His Word, Bible studies in large groups, Bible studies in small groups, and socializing with other believers. To a single mother with limited time, the idea of adding one more thing can be overwhelming. However, any single mother who is walking with Jesus will tell you that worshipping Him daily is a happy addition to their day.

> *This is the confidence we have in approaching God: that if we ask anything according to his will, he hears us.*
> —1 John 5:14

Just having the desire to be in communion with God is fantastic. Go one step further and make it a reality. When you are in communion with God and living according to His Word and His will, the world will not seem as daunting. Putting one foot in front of the other is the easiest way to begin. My personal search for growth in Christ came after I volunteered for Vacation Bible School to help teach five-year-olds. After I watched the children learn, understand, and comprehend the Trinity, my own pursuit of a relationship with Him was inevitable. It does not matter how you start—just start.

What are some of the first steps you can take to begin/revive your prayer life?

_____

_____

_____

_____

_____

_____

_____

_____

_____

_____

_____

_____

_____

_____

_____

_____

Digging Deeper with Scripture: 1 John 5:14; Matthew 6:9–13; Luke 11:9; 1 Timothy 2:1–10

How to Begin/Revive a Prayer Life

List prayers and thanksgiving for your child(ren).

List prayers and thanksgiving for yourself and what you have.

Idols

An idol is anything or anyone that captures your heart, mind, and affection more than God does. Idols are anything or anyone that you worship. Guess what? We all have them. If you are confused, look at where your money, time, and energy are directed. Idols are tricky because they're often disguised as good things such as children, a nice home, your career, or even marriage. Loving your children, advancing in your career, and working toward a great nest egg for retirement are all good things. However, when those things become your identity, you are idolizing them. God wants to be our *only* Lord and Savior, the only object of our worship. Be mindful of where you focus your time and attention.

> *The acts of the flesh are obvious: sexual immorality, impurity and debauchery; idolatry and witchcraft; hatred, discord, jealousy, fits of rage, selfish ambition, dissensions, factions and envy; drunkenness, orgies, and the like. I warn you, as I did before, that those who live like this will not inherit the kingdom of God. But the fruit of the Spirit is love, joy, peace, forbearance, kindness, goodness, faithfulness, gentleness and self-control. Against such things there is no law. Those who belong to Christ Jesus have crucified the flesh with its passions and desires.*
> —Gal. 5:19–24

As single mothers, we have the added issue of seeking and worshipping things we have little control over. Some of us worship the idea of marriage, a loving relationship, more free time, dependable or bigger cars, better careers, more money, and so on. Focusing on God's Word, His truth, and living in a Christlike manner make it easier for us to cast idols out of our lives. When we focus on God, we can't focus or fixate on our idols.

Can you identify the idols in your life? How can you begin to free yourself from the idols you have identified?

Digging Deeper with Scripture: Exodus 20:4; Deuteronomy 7:4; Jeremiah 5:19; Colossians 3:5

Idols

List prayers and thanksgiving for your child(ren).

List prayers and thanksgiving for yourself and what you have.

God's Gifts

I was in my late 40s when I realized my gifts from God were hospitality and encouragement. They showed up in ways such as praying over people, cooking for others or sharing a meal, and sending encouraging texts and emails. Often, I felt too tired to send a note, but I always had an incredible return on my investment when I ignored my discomfort and sent the encouragement in spite of my circumstances—when I listened to what God put on my heart and was obedient to His will.

My modeling this behavior has made a definite impression and imprint on my son when people come into our home. I have not spoken much on hospitality, yet he welcomes people into our home the same way I do. At this point in my life, sharing my gift with friends and family and showing my son what it means to be hospitable is most definitely a gift from God.

> *A gift opens the way and ushers the giver into the presence of the great.*
>
> —Prov. 18:16

Pray and ask God to reveal your gift to you. It is usually something that comes easily to you or takes little to no effort on your part. Whatever your gift—hospitality, discernment, prayer, teaching, leadership—there will be moments when the gift feels like a burden. There may be time when you won't want to take the assignment that God has given you. There may be other times when you will feel empty, with nothing else to give, and times when you feel you are not "prayed up" enough to pour out to another. God won't call the equipped, but He will equip the called. He knows that what you have to offer is life-giving.

Take some time to pray over and consider your spiritual gift. Now that you've identified it, how will it change the way you serve?

_____

_____

_____

_____

_____

_____

_____

_____

_____

_____

_____

_____

_____

_____

_____

_____

_____

Digging Deeper with Scripture: 1 John 5:14; Luke 11:9–10; 1 Thessalonians 5:17; Psalm 17:6; Matthew 6:9–13

God's Gifts

List prayers and thanksgiving for the people in your life.

List prayers and thanksgiving for the gift God has given you.

God's Gifts

List prayers and thanksgiving for your child(ren).

List prayers and thanksgiving for yourself and what you have.

Integrity

According to *Merriam-Webster*, *integrity* is a firm adherence to a code of especially moral or artistic values; it is incorruptibility. In the Bible, integrity is strongly associated with character and doing the right thing even when it is hard. I have an amazing coach, Sophia Casey, who sums up integrity quite well. She says, "Integrity is when what you believe, what you say, and what you do are all aligned." It is so tempting to cheat when no one is watching or to act a certain way with church friends and then revert to worldly ways at home or alone. Single mothers often live in two worlds: our Christian world and the fallen world. It may look like volunteering at church and then going out with friends and drinking too much or needing comfort and then sleeping with someone. What we do in secret will always come to the light. It is a tough line to tow as a single momma because your life feels so different from your married counterparts. And it is, but that does not mean that as a child of God, you get a different set of rules.

> *The integrity of the upright guides them, but the unfaithful are destroyed by their duplicity.*
> —Prov. 11:3

We must choose to live either in the fallen world or in Jesus. We cannot worship two masters. At some point, we will need to make a choice for our family. What will that choice be, and what will we choose?

In what ways can you practice integrity?

Digging Deeper with Scripture: 2 Kings 12:15; 1 Kings 9:4–5; Psalm 25:21; Proverbs 10:9

Integrity

List prayers and thanksgiving for your child(ren).

List prayers and thanksgiving for yourself and what you have.

Surrender to the Lord

Every athlete has a story about surrender—to a coach, a process, limitations, abilities—but there is always a surrender. Well, every Christian has a surrender story as well, a time when they cried out to Jesus Christ and asked him to be their personal Lord and Savior.

> *For all have sinned and fall short of the glory of God, and all are justified freely by his grace through the redemption that came by Christ Jesus.*
>
> —Rom. 3:23–24

If you have never asked for Jesus to come into your heart, repeat this prayer:

> *God, I have sinned against you, and I am deserving of punishment. Jesus took the punishment in my place so that I may have faith in Him and be forgiven. Please come into my heart and let me begin my personal relationship with Christ.*

Surrendering to our Lord can be so difficult for those who were not raised with Christ at the center of their lives or for those who believe they can do life on their own. Let me equate it to pregnancy to help you better understand what I mean by surrender. Pregnancy is a nine-month process. My pregnancy was rough. At 16 weeks, my sweet OB/GYN sat me down and told me about the rough road I was facing as a mom with preeclampsia. He sadly explained that 26 weeks was considered a safe time to deliver high-risk babies. I listened but felt no fear. The sweet, quiet voice in my head said, "We can do this!" I left that appointment determined that my pregnancy would end well and that my baby would not be delivered until he was strong enough to survive—and survive well—outside my body.

So, I surrendered my body to my son. It was his home, and he needed what my body could give him. I ate what I was supposed to. I kept my feet elevated above my heart at least six to eight hours a day. I rested. I worked part-time only, but I had money to pay bills. I was monitored weekly by my regular OB and a specialist. Mitchell was born at 30 weeks and one day, weighing 3.1 pounds. I felt safe, calm, and secure in that delivery room, not because I was surrounded by specialists, but because the One who is still a God of healing and miracles was in that room with us. We spent 40 days and nights in the NICU. My son was delivered early and safely because I surrendered my body to him when he needed it. It was easy to surrender to the Lord eighteen months later. Jesus is waiting for you to call His name and give everything to Him.

Surrender to the Lord

Have you ever surrendered your life to Jesus Christ? What did that look like?

_____

_____

_____

_____

_____

_____

_____

_____

_____

_____

_____

_____

_____

_____

_____

_____

_____

Digging Deeper with Scripture: Matthew 7:7, 16:24; Luke 9:23; Romans 6:23

List prayers and thanksgiving for your child(ren).

Surrender to the Lord

List prayers and thanksgiving for yourself and what you have.

List prayers and thanksgiving for the ability to surrender to Christ.

Serving

They say that 20 percent of the church does 80 percent of the work. Please consider being part of that 20 percent. The church is our spiritual family home and the cornerstone described in the New Testament. We should all consider serving joyfully. There are many ways to serve while our children are young. Many churches have nurseries; you can drop off your children while you serve. Serving can be as simple as being a greeter or serving coffee. Many ministries are not as time-consuming as you might think.

> *And whoever wants to be first must be slave of all. For even the Son of Man did not come to be served, but to serve, and to give his life as a ransom for many.*
> —Mark 10:44–45

The purpose of service is for God to reach others through you. God requires us to go out and make disciples of all nations. How beautiful it is to teach others the servant leadership of Christ through one's actions, to be used as God's instrument. God desires your service. Please don't be flippant and dismiss the church's call for help. We have all been served, and now we need to serve. Once the Lord has given you something, you should turn around and give it to another. It may not be your season, but when it is, serve as the Lord leads.

How can you, and even your child(ren), serve in the church this week, month, or year?

_____

_____

_____

_____

_____

_____

_____

_____

_____

_____

_____

_____

_____

_____

Digging Deeper with Scripture: Proverbs 11:25; 1 Peter 4:10; Galatians 6:10; Luke 6:35; Acts 20:35

SERVING

List prayers and thanksgiving for your child(ren).

List prayers and thanksgiving for yourself and what you have.

God First

We single mothers have a hard time imagining anything or anyone coming before our children. But God should come first. Such is the first and greatest commandment: "You shall have no other gods before me" (Exod. 20:3). God desires our time, attention, and obedience. He is our heavenly Father who sent His Son to die for our sins—that is, for the sins of people he would not know. He willingly sacrificed His life for us.

The idea of putting God first seems strange until you put it all into perspective. He gave and continues to give us all we have. Praising God should be automatic, but we get busy and focus on everything else but him. We forget who He is until we need something. Instead of looking at God as a last resort, why not elevate Him to number one? Before you go to bed, say thank you. When you open your eyes, say thank you. It takes 21 days to form a habit. After three weeks, it will become your norm. Thank and praise Him first thing in the morning and last thing at night and see where God ranks in your life a month from now—and note the change this will make.

> *But seek first the kingdom of God and his righteousness, and all these things will be added to you.*
> —Matt. 6:33 ESV

I remember when I started to put God first. It was hard for me to pick up my devotional and not to look at my phone first thing in the morning. Don't get me wrong: I still slip every now and then. But I found that giving God my first moments puts me in a more obedient and loving frame of mind. I find myself thinking through my conversations and the way I operate in the world. I find it easier and easier to go to God with everything. I have formed a habit of praising Him. I did not tell my son any of this, but he has started to follow suit. He started wanting me to play his Christian CDs and listen to the Christian radio station. Putting God first has not only changed my life, but it is changing my son's life. You will forever be changed too. I encourage you to take the leap. I have never regretted putting God before everything else in my life, including my child.

God First

List the things you are willing to give up in the morning to put God first. What things can you adopt to put Him first?

_____

Digging Deeper with Scripture: Matthew 22:37–40; Ephesians 1:22–23; Exodus 20:3; Psalm 27:6

List prayers and thanksgiving for your child(ren).

God First

List prayers and thanksgiving for yourself and what you have.

Acknowledgments

I give all glory to God for this creation. Left to my own devices, I would not have written or published this book. I would prefer to keep everything I write private.

I would like to thank my friends and family for their love and support during this process. Without them, I am positive this book would still be just a dream. A special shout-out to Sophia Casey, my cousin and international award-winning speaker, author, and executive coach. Girl, you have always shown up at the right time with the right words. Thank you for making me more authentic and helping me walk in integrity.

Thank you to my grandmother, who instilled a great sense of family and service in me through her example of tremendous sacrifices for her family. She has been gone for more than 20 years, yet it still feels like we lost her yesterday. Her legacy lives on.

A special thank you to my amazing uncle Kenny (may he rest in peace), who did not have a relationship with his biological father but became a father figure to us all. He taught us all the value of working hard, putting family first, and treating a lady with respect. At his funeral, we realized what a legacy he had built. This little girl loves you to the moon and back, and I miss you so much!

A special thank you to my mom, who was my first editor and spellchecker. She still harasses me over misspelled words and comma splices.

Thank you to Christopher, my unexpected gift, for loving me and staying by my side through all of this.

A huge thank you to the single mothers in my life who inspire me daily. I count myself privileged to watch you all care for your children, love each other and your families well, and still have time to give back.

Thank you all for being amazing women, mothers, coworkers, sisters in Christ, and friends.

Last, but certainly not least, thank you to my amazingly talented and beautiful cousin Irie. She raised a great young man, Idris, to adulthood after becoming a widow when he was a toddler. I admire your strength and courage. I have also been listening, watching, and taking notes. Yes, our children are worth the journey. I love you and appreciate you more than you know! Much peace!

Notes

Notes

Notes

NOTES

Notes

www.ingramcontent.com/pod-product-compliance
Lightning Source LLC
Chambersburg PA
CBHW060509090426
42735CB00011B/2155